# "Go See The Wizard"

### by
## Dr. William J. Keene

### Illustrations by
### Christy Karr

### Photography by
### Patricia Michel

Published and Distributed by
S&S
PO Box 1156
Torrance  CA  90505
(310) 375–0768

First Edition
First Printing
ISBN 0-9626914-3-7

Library of Congress Catalog Number

92-81715

Printed in the United States of America

# About The Author

On February ninth, 1992, William Keene was given an

 honorary doctorate of Religious Science by his church, presently located at 2244

Westwood Boulevard, Los Angeles. This was in recognition of meritorious service as a practitioner for a period of ninteen years. The material in this book introduces the reader to a few of the many extraordinary experiences encountered by workers in this particular field.

The Author of this treatise, when giving examples, has drawn from his own case files. He has been meticulous in disguising any individuals, so no one will be able to recognize those involved in any of the "case histories." The work of a Religious Science practitioner is as confidential and sacrosanct as the information received by the priest in the confessional.

# Contents

# Chapter I
# Beginnings

*Wherein the man finds his memory bringing back events that lead to his present work*

The man lay flat on his back staring out into his unlit bedroom. Not so much as a sliver of light impinged upon the total darkness. The only sound that reached his ears was the serene regularity of his wife's breathing as she lay sleeping at his side. The hour was close to midnight, a time which the man found to be ideal for his meditation, his prayerful work for his students, his "in absentia" treatments.

As a Religious Science practitioner he had many people for whom he did

Spiritual Mind treatments even though he might not see them from one month to the next, and much of his "midnight time" was usually devoted to such activity. Recently, however, he found himself thinking often of the various events that had lead him to his present professional activity. He realized that it had all started about 42 years ago.

He and his first wife were separated, but they maintained an amicable relationship; so when she asked him to "baby sit" one hot August afternoon, he said, "Sure." His son was not quite two, so could not be left alone. The man loved to spend time with the baby. The mother and the friend wanted to attend some kind of afternoon seminar.

When he arrived at the apartment, the two women were ready to leave at once. He looked in at the baby, who was sound asleep in his crib. "What a good idea!" the man thought. He stretched out on the living room sofa and dropped off to sleep almost immediately. He was not sure how long he slept, but he suddenly found himself in that limbo state - not fully awake, yet still not completely asleep. He was having a conversation with the Almighty!

The man was not a religious fanatic. This was, in fact, the first time he had experienced such a dream, but he was being very earnest and sincere in his request. "Make me a healer," he was saying. "I won't be 'holier than thou.' I'll talk very openly with the people who seek my help. No phoney-baloney spiel. I'll be very straight and up front with them. I'll be a good healer..." By this time he was awake.

Looking back through those years it is now very obvious that - at the time he requested it - the man was no more equipped for such activity than the proverbial "man in the moon." He needed a lot more living, a wider understanding of the "human condition," more reading of the metaphysical literature, more talks, seminars, church services, formal training through classes, expansion of consciousness.

He studied, he listened, he learned. He was enjoying a

career as an actor in those days. A subtle change began to take place in the kind of roles for which he was cast. He'd been doing largely "heavies" - now he started playing professional men, doctors, counselors, men of the cloth. He became town minister on a series that lasted eight years.

After he moved from New York to Los Angeles, he took up classes in earnest, earning his first year Religious Science certificate in 1971, second year certificate in 1972, third (the Practitioners course) in '73, and going on to take the somewhat longer fourth year with a certificate issued in June of 1975.

He had never been a "joiner," but after a year of attending an RSI church regularly, he became a member. Shortly thereafter he was asked to be President of the Mens Club, later a church usher, then Chief usher, then a member of the church Board, then Secretary of the Board.

It seems odd that - during this learning period - He didn't think about his earlier request to become a healer. What he was determined to do was to "be about his Father's business" and every new activity lead him in that specific direction.

As he moved forward in his study, he began to put various of the principles of the teaching to a test. The way they proved out was very impressive.

It was in his third year of formal class study that he experienced his first "demonstration." It came about in such a dramatic way that it caught him completely by surprise. The event changed his life.

# Chapter II
# Confirmation

*Spirit gives him his first powerful demonstration*

I It was in the fall 1972 that the man began his studies of third year Religious Science. When he completed this course he would be eligible to apply for his Practitioner's license.

He and the lady who would later become his wife had a ritual established. On mornings when they were both free they would meet at the Lake Hollywood Reservoir, walk and jog around the lake (under the famous Hollywood sign) and also do Spiritual Mind treatment. They were planning a trip - to drive across the country to

Michigan where the man had two sisters whom he had not seen for a very long time. A friend of theirs, an older woman by the name of Ann, became very intrigued with what they were doing.

"Just what do you do?" she asked.

"Well," the man replied, "when we're jogging, that's all we do. We're too short of breath to talk. When we're just walking, however, we treat."

"I've heard you use that word before," Ann said. "What, exactly, does that mean?"

"It's a lot like prayer, but differs in some important ways."

"Such as?"

"Most orthodox prayer involves begging, beseeching, imploring. The work we do affirms that what we are trying to bring about is already in the process of becoming our experience."

"Can you give me an example?"

"Sure. Let's say you need $500. The average person would look at his or her small bank balance and the few dollars in cash-on-hand and begin to worry. 'I'm never going to get that $500 in time to meet my obligation.' That sends precisely the wrong message to your indwelling Spirit. In Religious Science we say to that Spirit: 'I know that you are the source and substance of my good. I know you are aware of my requirements. I affirm that you are right now in the process of demonstrating my money. I give thanks and stand ready to receive my good.' That's a treatment and is followed by the appearance of the needed funds."

The man had many conversations with Ann on the subject. She was obviously very interested and she must have been discussing this with her friends. One warm, sunny Sunday afternoon after church the man and his lady were invited to a lawn party at Ann's home. There they met eight or ten people who were all fascinated by this somewhat unorthodox teaching.

They all asked a lot of questions, not based on idle curiosity, but very penetrating and intelligent. They all seemed particularly intrigued with the treatment process.

Finally the man decided the best approach would be to do a treatment for them. They were delighted at the prospect. One young woman even made a special request, "Would you please include in your treatment what you might say for a person who had a foreign object in his body that he wanted to get rid of."

The man promised to do so, and proceeded with a comprehensive treatment. This was followed by the serving of cookies and punch. Soon thereafter the party broke up. The following morning as the man was having his breakfast, the phone rang. It was Ann.

"You remember the woman who made the request yesterday?" she asked.

"Oh, sure."

"Well, I had a call from her this morning, and she was practically hysterical!"

"What happened?"

"I didn't know anything about this, but it seems that a week or ten days ago this woman [whom we'll call Margaret] had dropped and broken a glass in her kitchen.

She swept the floor and disposed of the broken pieces. Later in the day she had occasion to go to the kitchen for something and was in her bare feet. A shard of glass she had missed with her broom was driven into her heel. She was in agony. Her doctor had her come to his office where he removed the glass and bandaged her foot. Later that day she realized he hadn't gotten it all out. When she came to our party yesterday, she still had the problem. Her request was really a cry for help."

"What brought on the hysterics?" the man asked.

"The way she told it to me this morning," Ann replied, "while you were treating yesterday, Margaret began to feel a warm sensation in the heel of her foot. This feeling continued after the party broke up. She went home and propped herself up in bed and was reading a good book. Suddenly she felt what she referred to as a 'drawing feeling.' It was so pronounced that she pulled the bedcovers back to look, and there was a sliver of glass sticking out of her heel! She had some tweezers on her bedside table which she used to remove the glass, and her problem was solved."

The story had a profound effect on the man. First of all, since he had no prior knowledge of Margaret's problem, it was, therefore, not a case of the mind of the giver of the treatment working to correct (heal) the condition of the recipient. The practitioner's absolute conviction of perfection generated an action on the part of the recipient's spirit that caused the ejection of the "foreign object."

The second and more important result was that the giver's spirit demonstrated that spiritual power was available for healing purposes and it was willing to work for the practitioner to produce desired results.

This caused the man to feel that he had received "a call," and he immediately determined to complete the third year course and apply for his license. That license was issued to him in the fall of 1973.

# Chapter III
# No Human Condition

*A cancer case very early in his career brings conviction*

The man was unmarried at the time he began his practice. His apartment also served as his office. He had a few regular students almost from the beginning. Others came to him through his church affiliation or by word of mouth. Early in his career a young lady asked for an appointment and came in for an in-person session.

"I'm not here expecting you to perform a miracle," the young lady said. "I've just come from visiting my father in the hospital. He's lying there in agony, out of his head. My problem is that my father has recently married again, is living with his young wife, has very young children by her, and has not made any provisions for them. I've got to have an intelligent conversation with him so that those youngsters will be taken care of, if anything happens to him."

"What does the doctor tell you about your father's condition?"

"He has an inoperable cancer that is wrapped around his spinal column. No surgery can be performed.

Nobody can judge the time element."

"All right," the man said, "what you and I must affirm is that we do not have to accept the verdict. Realize that the doctor sees all things through a medical frame of reference, his entire training is based on that knowledge. What he is telling you is what his vision is trained to see and analyze. You and I can accept the presence of a higher power that sees perfection. We'll generate action on the part of that spirit and dissolve the appearance."

The man then proceeded to give a very potent treatment. The young woman understood the procedure and accepted the work that was done. As they parted company at the end of the session, she said, "I'll see you in church."

They did indeed meet in church the following Sunday, and the young lady took the man somewhat by surprise. She embraced him and planted a kiss on his cheek!

"I went to see my father the very next day after our session," she said. "He was sitting up in bed enjoying a good lunch! We've had our talk, he's arranging things for the youngsters, and I can't tell you how grateful i am for your work."

"My dear," the man explained, "the work was done by Spirit. I'm only a catalytic agent. There is no human condition that cannot be healed through spiritual mind treatment. I believe that with all my heart. Otherwise, I would be a charlatan."

The young lady made an appointment for later that week, but on that day she called to change the date. "I can't keep my time with you," she explained. "I'm driving my father home from the hospital today!"

The family moved to another part of the state later that year, but five years later the young woman showed up unexpectedly at church one Sunday. The man was delighted to see her. "How's your father?" he asked.

"Just fine!"

# Chapter IV
# Good Is All There Is

*The man dissolved a deep-rooted superstition to free a student from witchcraft*

I n the beginning the man used his little bachelor apartment as his office. One morning as he was finishing breakfast his phone rang. A woman's voice with strong elements of distress in it asked him if he had any time available in the near future. The man looked in his appointment book and said, "I can see you at 3 o'clock this afternoon."

"Wonderful," the woman exclaimed, got instructions on how to get there, and hung up.

A few minutes before three there was a tap on his door. The woman was very attractive, black, and quite obviously in a state of distress. When they were both seated, the man asked her to explain the problem. "I am being subjected to witchcraft! You've got to help me!"

This was certainly a new kind of challenge. The man said, "Will you run that past me one more time?" The woman repeated her statement. "I just wanted to be sure I understood you correctly. It's a rather unusual case. Please tell me about it."

"I live in what is largely a Haitian neighborhood. I moved there about a month ago. I make friends rather slowly, and this is sometimes mistaken as snobbishness. Suddenly, strange things began to happen. I would be awakened in the night by a pounding on my door. When I'd check it out, there would be nobody in sight. I'd go out to pick up my newspaper in the morning and there would be a little gift-wrapped package on top of the paper. When I got in the house and opened the little box, there would be a dead bird in it. This sort of thing continued.

"One day a woman came to my door. 'I live just a few

doors down the street,' she told me. 'I need a friend to come and do my housework. I was told you might be that person.' I'm sorry, I told her, someone has given you the wrong information. I don't do housework. 'How strange!' and the woman looked at me in a peculiar way. 'My source of information is always very reliable. Perhaps you should reconsider.' She turned quickly and walked way.

Shortly after that I began to feel a strong pull coming from that woman's house. I would awake in the night, having dreamed that I was working as the woman's maid. Somehow, my thoughts don't seem to belong to me anymore!"

It was obvious to the man that certain people in her neighborhood were practicing voodoo, a kind of power sometimes called "obeah." In modern parlance they were "putting a whammy on her." It was, of course, all nonsense, but to a receptive mind steeped in ancient superstition it could appear very threatening. The man talked with her, attempting to establish a good rapport. When he felt she trusted him he explained about Spiritual Mind treatment and began to work toward the clarification of her thinking.

The process required six or seven visits, during which time the woman began attending Sunday services at the man's church. He could see a good change taking place. Finally one Sunday he saw her walking toward him where he was stationed at the entrance to the sanctuary. He knew the moment that he saw her that she was over her problem. "You're free!" he said grinning. She grinned right back and said, "I sure am."

At that time the man was Chief Usher, so he helped in the collection and went upstairs later to help with the counting. When he came down it was usually about a half hour after the end of the service. On this day, the lady was waiting for him.

"I just had to tell you how very much I appreciate what you've done for me."

"My dear lady," the man said, "it was really your spirit that made the change."

"You taught me that 'God, the good, is all there is.' You made me see that if something is not good, it is not of God - therefore it is a lie. If it has no basis in truth, I (being one with God's good) don't have to deal with it."

"Absolutely correct. But you saw that truth, you accepted it, and you allowed it to set you free!" She had been a good student. The man expected her to continue attending church on Sundays, but that didn't happen. He said good-bye to her on that day and never saw her again!

# Chapter V
# Enter The Wizard

## *A group of young students nominate the man for a unique title*

N aturally, the man's students changed from time to time. Actors went out with road shows, people moved way, there was an almost constant exchange of times. There was one period when the man had a large number of

 young people as students. He had discovered early in his practitioning that 20 students a week was about the maximum he could handle effectively for in-person

sessions and those appointments, coupled with his in absentia treatments (usually conducted in the mornings), were what he felt best able to accommodate. Of the 20 students during the period referred to, sixteen were women between 18 and 31 years of age, mostly in their early 20's and quite lovely. After he had been seeing them for a while. one day one of them said, "We've got a new name for you."

"Oh?" The man was intrigued. "May I know what my new name is?"

"Sure!" The young woman smiled. "We've decided you're the Wizard of OZ!"

He grinned. "I like that a lot. First of all, when I was a youngster, L. Frank Baum was in his heyday. He wrote a dozen or so "OZ" stories, and after he passed on, a young lady (I think it was his niece) wrote several more. I could hardly wait for each new book to come out.

"Then, of course, I always loved Frank Morgan and felt his characterization of the Wizard in the movie was outstanding."

"Well," my young student said, "we have this little group and when any one of us has a problem to deal with we say 'Go see the Wizard!'"

"I've been meaning to ask you," the man said, "how is it that so many of you seem to know each other?"

The lady gave him a quizzical look. "You mean you don't know?"

"Not really," the man replied. "Why does my not knowing surprise you?"

"You're a pretty sophisticated man," the woman answered. "I thought you'd have figured it out by now."

"Suppose you tell me," he suggested.

"About seven of us are call girls!" came the surprising answer!

The practitioner continued to see the members of this "family" for the better part of a year. It is probably well to point out that an individual who has taken the classes necessary to become a practitioner must set aside all prejudice, all judgemental attitudes. All humans are expressions of one Presence, one Power, one Life Force, one Infinite Intelligence. If we show disapproval for any person because of religion, color of skin, sexual preference, or

any other of the thoughtless
reasons for discriminating
against our fellow creatures, we
are questioning the wisdom of
Almighty God.

The slogan of "Go see the
Wizard" struck the man as an
excellent title for a book. Thus,
over a period of time, the ideas
you are presently reading began
to move toward forming these
Chapters.

# Chapter VI
# The "Instant Breakfast" Treatment

## *The man devises a general treatment to establish spiritual identity and power*

Everyone is acquainted with the commercial product that has in its title the words "Instant Breakfast." It's a powder to which you add milk, fruit juice or whatever, and it provides a highly nutritional drink that gets your body charged up first thing in the morning.

As a Religious Science practitioner, the man thought there should be some kind of spiritual "shot in the arm" that would accomplish the same thing at the level of consciousness that the drink does at the physical level.

His work kept him in contact with Spirit on a pretty consistent basis, and he knew the power of Spirit-Mind action; he was not in the least surprised when a treatment began to formulate in his head.

The most common challenge facing the people who came to the man for his practitioning help was their lack of understanding as to who and what they really were. Oh, they were acquainted with the individual that expressed between the top of their head and the tips of their toes, but the spiritual entity that lived inside that body was an enigma. Most student's didn't have a clue.

"The first thing you need is to start your students thinking about their real identity," his intuition told him. Little by little the first paragraph of the treatment presented itself to him. It wasn't complicated but it held a very powerful truth. It read as follows - "I willing, joyfully, enthusiastically accept my correct identity as God being me." Now, there are many people who have difficulty in accepting the idea that they are individual expressions of the Almighty, but until they are willing to take that step, they are deliberately cutting themselves off from their good.

The second paragraph reads as follows: "I right now instruct the little human ego-self of me to stand aside, and I call forth from the very center of my being my true God-self, affirming that that will *do* the expressing for me throughout this day!" This declaration specifically calls upon the inner spirit to take over, which means that the human individual who has made that affirmation will now be expressed by means of God qualities. It doesn't get any better than that. Every student who came to "The Wizard" more than once has a copy of the "Instant Breakfast Treatment."

It is recommended that the student keep a copy of the treatment at his or her bedside. The moment you realize you're awake and ready to begin another day, use the treatment. It is guaranteed to put your "spiritual train" on the track. What you are being given is a kind of "Aladdin's Lamp."

The man has students who, although they very definitely believe in the teaching, can't seem to make it work for them. When asked how they are doing with the "Instant Breakfast Treatment," they look out the window and do a lot of hemming and hawing.

"You're not using it, are you?"

"Well, I haven't gotten into the habit as yet."

"If you don't rub the lamp, the genie will not appear, and your wishes will not be granted."

USE THE TREATMENT. Use it every morning. If you need it again later in the day, use it. It won't wear out - AND IT WORKS!

# Chapter VII
# The Canopy of Divine Right Action

*A treatment designed for a particular individual's needs proves to be a powerful spiritual concept for everyone*

The title for this chapter is the man's name for another treatment of great spiritual power. He almost stumbled into the idea, although he knows that, in truth, all ideas come from Spirit. One of his students was planning a trip to France. It was to combine a vacation with some specific business activities.

The man devised a concept that was intended to cause all aspects of her trip to work with remarkable smoothness. It was designed to cause her to make all her connections with time to spare, no experiences of loss of luggage, all reservations confirmed, all meetings resulting in total success, good health, total peace of mind, adequate funds to afford the very best, etc.

This practitioner always had excellent results from the Visualization Process, (see chapter VIII) so he described his idea to his student. The canopy was like a large lawn umbrella, but, because it was a spiritual concept, it had certain unusual features.

It had no center pole! She, the student, was the equivalent of that pole, since the canopy always floated directly over her head. It seemed as though there was nothing between the circular canopy and the ground, but there was an invisible screen that went from the circumference of the umbrella-like structure right to the floor or ground or whatever surface the student walked or stood upon.

The canopy went wherever the woman went. It had the ability to expand or contract according to the require-ments of the moment. Nobody could see it except the stu-dent and her practitioner when they chose to do so. The screen had special qualities - anything and everything that contributed to the enrichment and enhancement of the woman's life was free to enter through the screen and join her under the canopy. However, all things negative, destructive and violent were completely unable to penetrate the screen and were instantly deflected at the moment of contact.

It was a remarkably powerful and effective spiritual concept, and the practitioner felt very good about providing his student with such an all-inclusive aura of protection.

When the young lady had been in Paris for about two weeks, she felt prompted to call "The Wizard." "I don't fully understand what you've done," she told him, "but whatever it is - KEEP ON DOING IT! Everything is working perfectly. I have met with all my business associates, I have made some valuable new contacts, both business and social. As my reserved time at the place where I'm staying is running out, I've found some people who are leaving for Los

Angeles, so we've made arrangements for them to use my apartment there and I am moving into their home here right after their departure. I've even been offered a job in Paris if I want it!"

It is exactly the kind of confirmation that has moved this practitioner from faith to absolute "knowingness."

# Chapter VIII
# Visualization

*A God-given talent becomes a valuable tool to generate demonstration*

W e have already
touched on the
power of
visualization in Chapter VII. It
consists in using one's
imagination to see certain

pictures,
ideas and
impressions
in what we
sometimes call "The Mind's
Eye." When we have accepted
the truth - that what we

permit to
take place
in the inner
world of our

consciousness is the
causative force that
structures the world of our

experience -the visualization process takes on a much greater importance. It can, in a very literal sense, become a means of controlling what we desire to demonstrate in our life expression.

Let's use the demonstration of money as an example, since many people have managed to persuade themselves that money is a big problem in their lives.

Visualization #1: Close your eyes and see before you a little table, about the size of a so-called "end table." On this table are two stacks of American currency. Reach out and pick up one of these stacks. A quick inspection reveals that each bill is of the denomination of $1,000. You riffle through the stack and conclude that there are 50 bills - you are now holding in one hand $50,000! Now you examine the paper tape that holds the bills together. On that tape is imprinted your name! Now, you pick up the other stack and easily recognize that it is exactly the same as the first. You are now holding in your two hands $100,000! And your name is on the money! You can take it home!

What, exactly, are we doing? We are strengthening, expanding, developing your money consciousness. I am fully aware that there are many people in this world who will say, "Poppycock!" If you are willing to listen to them, you'll never practice the exercise, and you'll never know what it's capable of doing for you.

Does it work? "The Wizard" had a man who came to him and said "I am desperate. I don't have any food money for the next week. I'm not going to be able to pay my rent. I don't know where to turn." They practiced Spiritual Mind treatment, and six months later the man was asking for the name of a good business manager to handle his money for him!

You have only been given one example of visualization. There are, of course, many more. The secret is to alter the attitude you have toward the subject of money. A new consciousness of the principal that governs your supply will open all the channels of receptivity for you. In the same way you can use the power of visualization to produce other good things in your life - health, happiness, peace, love, order, success, creativity.

Remember - what you allow in the inner world of your consciousness is the causative force that structures the world of your experience.

# Chapter IX
# Self-Esteem

*The most important item on the spiritual agenda has strong validation*

We have all known people who have gone through this country's educational system, have graduated from good colleges with honor, and still have never achieved any real success. We have also known (or read about, or heard of) people who have come from very modest origins, had to scratch to get any kind of acceptable education, and have risen to great heights.

What sets the successful people apart? It is a quality called self-esteem. It is the individual's ability to believe in himself or herself, and to carry the absolute conviction that all seeming obstacles can be (and will be) overcome.

Can every individual achieve this all-important spiritual power? Yes! Do all people achieve it? No! Why is that? Because many people have little or no faith in themselves. Worse than that, they lack belief in the presence within them of a "higher power."

Let's try to take an objective view of ourselves and find a logical process for accepting the availability of personal self-esteem.

If you live and move and have your being, that means that you have what all humans have - specifically, God's stamp of approval. Without that, you simply would not exist. The Almighty has okayed you as a point in His total expression. This also means that you have His love. That love is unconditional - no strings attached. This relationship exists between God and every living human, whether the individual knows it or not. The truth applies even when it's not recognized.

Now, if that is true (and it is), then does it not logically follow that you are authorized to approve of yourself? Of course it does! If Almighty God approves of you, does it matter if your neighbor does or does not think highly of you? Do you need a passing grade from all of the people in the world? Isn't it true that if the power that created you (and the cosmos) thinks of you as A-#1, you have everything you need. Yes! Believe that every great idea that comes to you is spiritually generated and it is therefore spiritually supported. You can be as successful as you want to be!

# Chapter X
# The Cosmic
# Experiment

## *Why we need God and why God needs us*

"In the beginning," we are told, "all was void." Within that void, however, existed a Presence. It was formless and invisible. It was a vast Mind, and that mind engaged in self-contemplation. Thus, through the Law, was projected into form the cosmos and everything in it. It was not, however, until that great Universal Intelligence created humankind that it saw a way in which it could actually have the experience of finite life - without losing its established identity as a formless and invisible entity.

It accomplished this by individualizing itself as the indwelling Spirit of each living human. You are, I am, each one of us is, God finding out what it's like to be alive as us. Without the presence of God in you, you would be nothing. You wouldn't exist. You depend upon God as the source of your life. Furthermore, since God, the Good, is all there is, that presence is the source and substance of all your good. Every good thing that has ever happened to you is the result of some action on the part of your indwelling Spirit.

The human condition being what it is, we are immediately prompted to ask, "What about all the not-so-good things? Where do they come from?"

We all accept the fact that there is a lot that is negative in our finite world - the world of appearances. We can be constant witnesses to violence, destructive elements, all the things that make up what I call the "garbage of the material world." When we know that we are - each of us - individual expressions of God, we also come to realize that we really

don't have to do business
with the "garbage."

Let me
give you a
picture of
the way this
"cosmic
experiment"
works, based
on our understanding of
computers. Imagine yourself
as a computer that records
everything that happens to
you as a human individual.
This data is then relayed to
the "master computer" - the
Mind of God. While that is
going on, relative to your life,
the 'master computer' is

receiving data from all the other computers on this planet, recording it, categorizing it, and filing it for immediate reference whenever desired. In this way, the mind of God has carefully stored within Itself a detailed account of all human experience. This experiment has been going on since God created the human race, and each one of us is part of the total information. Apparently the system is entirely satisfactory to the Almighty, since it is still functioning.

Keeping in mind that God is a formless and invisible

entity, we can see that this Spirit needs a vehicle to get around on a finite plane. We are that vehicle to our own personal indwelling Spirit. It needs an instrumentation for purposes of expression. We are that instrumentation.

We, therefore, are important to God as He individualizes Himself (Herself, itself) in us. He sees us as valuable, worthy, deserving.

When you are treating, affirm that your indwelling spirit is willingly taking whatever action is needed to make you the best, the most effective instrument you can possibly be. "Seek ye first the kingdom of heaven [within yourself] and all these things [the joys of living] will be added unto you."

START TODAY! If you need help, there are a lot of "Wizards" available!